Mako Sharks

Victoria Blakemore

vblakemore.author@gmail.com

Copyright info/picture credits

Cover, prochym/AdobeStock; Page 3, wildestanimal/ Shutterstock; Page 5, prochym/AdobeStock; Page 7, prochym/AdobeStock; Page 9, dimitrivetsikas1969/Pixabay; Pages 10-11, Fotoworkshop4you/Pixabay; Page 13, Matthew R. McClure/AdobeStock; Page 15, prochym/AdobeStock; Page 17, Alessandro De Maddalena/Shutterstock; Page 19, Marc/AdobeStock; Page 21, Marc/AdobeStock; Page 23; prochym/AdobeStock; Page 25, wildestanimal/AdobeStock; Page 27, prochym/AdobeStock; Page 29, kitti bowornphatnon/AdobeStock; Page 31, Marc/AdobeStock; Page 33, Alessandro De Maddalena/Shutterstock

Table of Contents

What Are Mako Sharks?

Mako sharks are large fish. They are from the same family as great white sharks.

There are two kinds of mako sharks: the shortfin mako and the longfin mako. The shortfin mako is the most common kind.

Mako sharks are gray with a white belly. They sometimes look blue depending on the light.

Size

Mako sharks grow very quickly compared to other sharks. They often grow to be about thirteen feet long.

Adult mako sharks often weigh between 150 and 300 pounds. Larger mako sharks have been seen, but they are not as common.

Female mako sharks are

usually larger than male

mako sharks.

Physical Characteristics

Mako sharks have a long, thin body. The shape of their body is very **streamlined**. It allows them to swim at very fast speeds.

Unlike most other sharks, mako sharks are warm-blooded. Their body stays warmer than the water around them.

Mako sharks have a white underside. When seen from below, it can blend in with the water's surface.

7

Habitat

Mako sharks are found in most oceans. They are usually found far out in the ocean. They do not come close to **shore**.

They are best suited to the open ocean because of the large fish they prey on.

Range

Mako sharks are found in the Atlantic, Pacific, and Indian oceans.

The only ocean where mako sharks are not found is the Arctic ocean. It is too cold.

Diet

Mako sharks are **carnivores**.

They only eat meat.

Their diet is made up of fish like tuna or bluefish. They may also eat dolphins, smaller sharks, squid, and sea turtles. They often eat whatever they are able to catch.

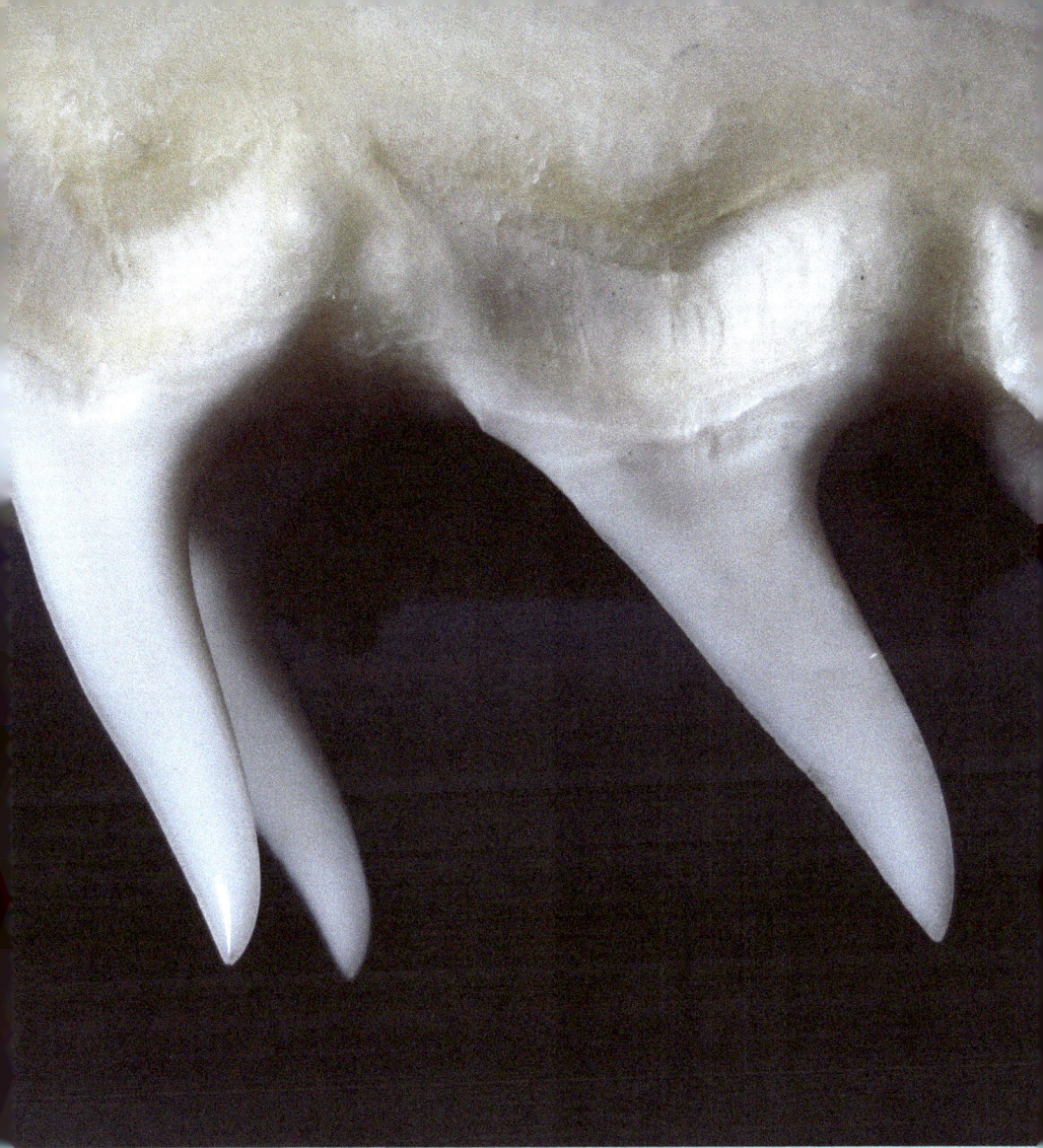

Mako teeth are long, thin, and

sharp. They are so long that they

stick out of the shark's mouth.

Mako sharks are very good hunters. Their speed helps them to catch prey easily. They often come up from under their prey to catch it by surprise.

They swim so fast that they have been known to **launch** themselves completely out of the water while chasing prey.

The color of a mako shark's skin

can work as **camouflage**. It

helps them to blend in to the

dark waters. **15**

Communication

Mako sharks do not use sound to communicate with each other. Most of their communication seems to be through movement.

Mako sharks have a special movement pattern before some attacks. They may swim in a figure eight pattern before they attack.

Mako sharks often charge at their prey. Swimming towards something at high speeds could show **aggression**.

Movement

Their tail is shaped like a tuna's tail and is very powerful. This allows them to swim very quickly in a forward direction.

They have been known to swim as fast as 60 miles per hour. This is much faster than many other sharks.

Shortfin mako sharks are the world's fastest sharks. Their speed makes them good hunters.

Mako Shark Life

Mako sharks are **solitary**. They spend most of their time alone. They are very rarely seen in groups.

They are typically found out in the open ocean and are rarely seen close to the **coast**. They may travel long distances while hunting.

The mako shark's speed makes it dangerous to humans. However, they prefer the open ocean, far from where most people swim.

Mako Shark Pups

Mako sharks usually have

between 4 and 20 babies.

Their babies are called pups.

The pups are usually born in

late winter or early spring. They

are often about twenty-eight

inches long when they are

born.

Pups are on their own right after they are born. They do not stay with their mother.

Lifespan

In the wild, mako sharks may live as long as 35 years. They do not do well in **captivity**.

The few times that mako sharks have been kept at aquariums, they have only lived for a few days. They need more space than an aquarium can give them.

Mako sharks live about as long

as most other sharks in the wild.

They need to be in the open

ocean, not in **captivity**.

Population

Mako shark populations have been **declining** in recent years. They are hunted for their meat and fins. They are also sometimes caught in fishing lines and nets by mistake.

Longfin mako sharks are **endangered**. There are not many left in the wild.

Shortfin mako sharks are listed

as **vulnerable**. They may soon

be **endangered**.

Mako Sharks in Danger

Like many other sharks, mako sharks are hunted for their fins, meat, and hides.

Many times, they are caught only for their fins, which are used in shark fin soup. Their fins are used to add **texture** to the soup.

Shark fin soup is a **delicacy** in some countries. The soup is made from the fins of sharks like mako sharks.

Helping Mako Sharks

There are laws that protect sharks from being caught for their fins.

People are educating others about shark fins and products that have shark oil. They are trying to keep sharks from being hunted.

The United States has set limits on how many mako sharks may be caught. The hope is that other countries will try to protect mako sharks too.

Special conservation zones are areas that are protected from fishing and hunting sharks. They provide sharks with a safe habitat.

Glossary

Aggression: the use of force, shows that the animal is ready to fight

Camouflage: using color to blend in to the surroundings

Captivity: when an animal is kept by humans, not in the wild

Carnivore: an animal that eats only meat

Coast: the area where land meets the ocean

Declining: getting smaller

Delicacy: a food that is rare and special

Endangered: at risk of becoming extinct

Launch: to move with force

Shore: the land beside the ocean

Solitary: living without others, alone

Streamlined: smooth, rounded surface that allows for fast movement through water

Texture: the feel or look of a surface

Vulnerable: an animal that is likely to become endangered

About the Author

Victoria Blakemore is a first grade

teacher in Southwest Florida with a

passion for reading.

You can visit her at

www.elementaryexplorers.com

Also in This Series

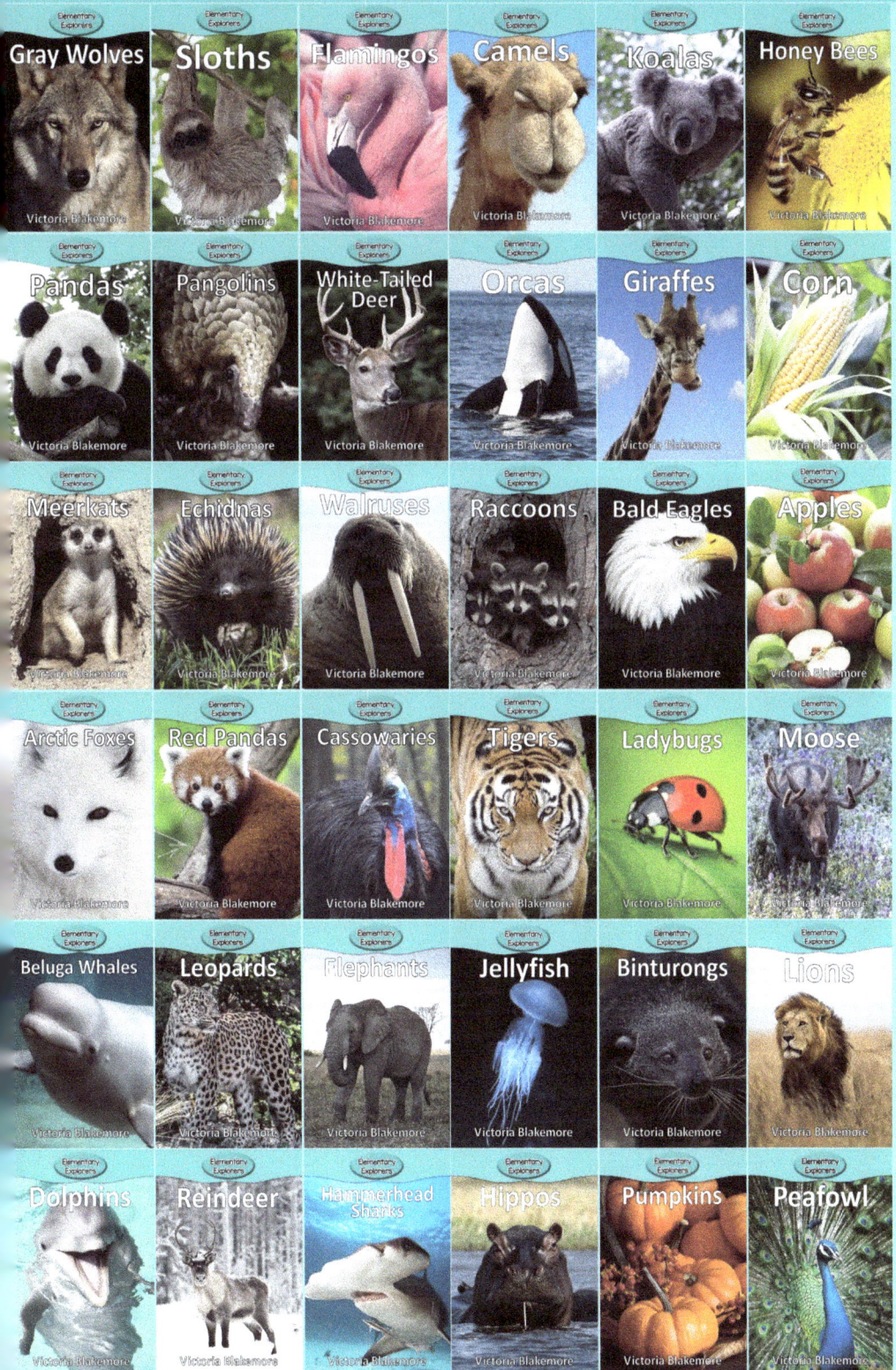

Gray Wolves	**Sloths**	**Flamingos**
Victoria Blakemore	Victoria Blakemore	Victoria Blakemore
Camels	**Koalas**	**Honey Bees**
Victoria Blakemore	Victoria Blakemore	Victoria Blakemore
Pandas	**Pangolins**	**White-Tailed Deer**
Victoria Blakemore	Victoria Blakemore	Victoria Blakemore
Orcas	**Giraffes**	**Corn**
Victoria Blakemore	Victoria Blakemore	Victoria Blakemore
Meerkats	**Echidnas**	**Walruses**
Victoria Blakemore	Victoria Blakemore	Victoria Blakemore
Raccoons	**Bald Eagles**	**Apples**
Victoria Blakemore	Victoria Blakemore	Victoria Blakemore
Arctic Foxes	**Red Pandas**	**Cassowaries**
Victoria Blakemore	Victoria Blakemore	Victoria Blakemore
Tigers	**Ladybugs**	**Moose**
Victoria Blakemore	Victoria Blakemore	Victoria Blakemore
Beluga Whales	**Leopards**	**Elephants**
Victoria Blakemore	Victoria Blakemore	Victoria Blakemore
Jellyfish	**Binturongs**	**Lions**
Victoria Blakemore	Victoria Blakemore	Victoria Blakemore
Dolphins	**Reindeer**	**Hammerhead Sharks**
Victoria Blakemore	Victoria Blakemore	Victoria Blakemore
Hippos	**Pumpkins**	**Peafowl**
Victoria Blakemore	Victoria Blakemore	Victoria Blakemore

Elementary Explorers

Also in This Series

Chameleons	Florida Panthers	Aye-Ayes	Black Bears	Cheetahs	Manatees
Gingerbread	Polar Bears	Hot Chocolate	Orangutans	Coyotes	Marshmallows
Strawberries	Aardvarks	Mako Sharks	Alligators	Frogs	Hedgehogs
Brown Bears	Bongos	Sea Turtles	Quokkas	Muskrats	Zebras
Red Foxes	Ring-Tailed Lemurs	Platypuses	Anteaters	Kangaroos	Rhinos
Jaguars	Wombats				

All titles by Victoria Blakemore, Elementary Explorers.